Seymour School Library
East Granby, Conn.

What the World Eats

EVENING MEAL

TOM AND JENNY WATSON

CHILDRENS PRESS INTERNATIONAL

What the World Eats

Breakfast
Midday Meal
Evening Meal

Library of Congress Cataloging in Publication Data
Watson, Tom.
Evening meal.

(What the world eats)
Bibliography: p.
Includes index.
Summary: Describes the evening habits of people in all parts of the world and the foods they choose to eat, as well as how they grow or shop for their food and prepare their evening meal.
1. Dinners and dining—Juvenile literature. 2. Food habits—Juvenile literature. 3. Cookery, International—Juvenile literature. [1. Dinners and dining. 2. Food habits] I. Watson, Jenny. II. Title. III. Series: Watson, Tom. What the world eats.
TX737.W33 1983 394.1'5   82-19909
ISBN 0-516-01858-2

**1983 American Edition published by
Childrens Press International**

© Copyright 1982 Wayland Publishers Ltd, England

Phototypeset by Direct Image,
Hove, East Sussex
Printed in Italy by G. Canale & C.S.p.A., Turin
Bound in the U.S.A.

Contents

1	WHAT WE EAT IN ENGLAND AND THE UNITED STATES	4
	High tea in England	6
	Dinner	8
	Why we eat these things	11
	Special occasions	12
	Eating out	14
	How food is preserved	16
	How and where we buy food	18
	Breaking the code	20
2	WHAT PEOPLE IN OTHER COUNTRIES EAT	22
	Germany	24
	Hungary	26
	Spain	28
	Soviet Union	31
	Israel	32
	Saudi Arabia	34
	Sudan	36
	Nigeria	38
	Morocco	40
	India	42
	Malaysia	45
	China	46
	Chile	49
	Brazil	50
	Recipes	52
3	FOOD FOR LIFE: HYGIENE	54
	Feast and famine	56
	The results of eating	58

Glossary	60
Finding out more	62
Index	63

1 · What we eat

The evening meal comes at the end of the day when people have finished at work or school. Evening is a time for people to sit down, enjoy their meal, and relax. The time at which the evening meal is eaten varies from family to family. For some the last meal of the day may be early; for others it may be a late meal—a supper—or something eaten in the middle of the evening. The time people eat their meal often depends on when the family comes home. Those who live near their work can, if they wish, eat early. In other families someone may have to travel a long distance and not be home till late—evening meals in these homes must be enjoyed at a later hour.

People prefer different types of food for their evening meal, and often choose to eat their food in different surroundings. Some may like a light supper in front of the television, others a more substantial meal at the table. In sunnier countries, meals can be eaten out of doors: a table is set up outside or there may be a barbecue in the garden. Many people enjoy barbecuing steaks and chops over an open fire. In some parts of the world, it is not just on special occasions that whole families will enjoy their main meal of the day in a restaurant. What do you usually eat for your evening meal?

Right *Eating out-of-doors— two boys wait for their meal of barbecued hamburgers and hot dogs.*

Below *Because many families like to watch television while they eat, their evening meal may be eaten from trays.*

High tea in England

In England high tea is usually eaten early in the evening, between five o'clock and six o'clock. People may eat many different things at this time. For some it is a fairly substantial meal, but others prefer a lighter meal, often because they will be eating again later—many people like a snack supper before they go to bed.

For those who like a fairly large meal, high tea usually begins with a hot savory dish, such as fish sticks, hamburgers, sausages, egg, baked beans, or spaghetti. Chips (french fries), too, are always popular. In the summer, salads are often served instead. This will be followed by a sweet dish—perhaps jelly, ice cream, or trifle (sponge cake). Cakes and sweet breads are traditional tea-time foods, especially popular with members of the family who have a sweet tooth. There may be toasted tea cakes or crumpets (toasted muffins) served with butter and jam, and buttered fruit loaf or iced rolls. There may also be a choice from a selection of cakes, such as a slice of fruit, plain or iced cake, or perhaps a small cake or roll.

A lighter meal may consist of bread and jam or sandwiches, and cakes. Many people drink tea with this meal, though the younger members of the family may prefer a glass of milk or fruit soda.

Left *Two popular toasted treats for tea — crumpets and Eastertime hot cross buns.*

Above *Chocolate cake is a favorite in many homes — here Mother decorates a freshly-baked cake for tea-time.*

Dinner

Families who eat dinner—some call it supper—usually eat between 5 P.M. and 7 P.M. The traditional dinner is meat, potatoes, and another vegetable. Good meat has for long been thought of as the most important part of the meal. Usually, because of its high quality, it has not been masked with highly-flavored sauces; rather it has been served simply roasted, boiled, fried, or broiled.

With meat heading the family cook's list of priorities, vegetables have been looked upon largely as the part of the meal that fills you up. Because of this, some people do not take care to cook them carefully. Vegetables only need to be cooked for a short time so that they do not lose their flavor and become limp. It is important, too, not to overcook them, as this destroys their vitamin content.

Now, with more people going abroad for their holidays and with more people from foreign countries making their home in our country, our dinner often contains a dish from another

Left Meat usually forms an important part of the meal. Here beef carcasses are being inspected for quality.

Above An extraspecial dinner for sharing with friends.

country—lasagna from Italy, curry from India, or goulash from Hungary. The potato, which provides us with most of our vitamin C, often gives up its place to pasta, rice, or beans.

After their main course, many families eat a dessert—a fruit pie or tart, or perhaps an 'instant' dessert. Those who prefer to finish their meal with a more nutritious dish, instead of satisfying a sweet tooth, are more likely to round off their dinner with a little cheese and some fresh fruit.

Why we eat these things

Most healthy people are hungry before a meal and have a good appetite. If a dish smells and tastes particularly good, we might eat more than usual. Extra herbs are added when we cook stews and casseroles so that our food will have a more appealing taste and smell when we eat it.

We will also enjoy our food more if it is presented attractively on the plate. Here, the colors of the various ingredients attract our eye as well as our palate. This can be easily achieved with the simplest of meals: plain roast or grilled meat can be made more tempting to the eye if it is served on the same plate with vegetables of different colors—some green cabbage, orange carrots, and white potatoes, for example. If you had a plate of white fish, white potatoes, and white cauliflower, it would not *look* especially tempting to eat.

We should also take care to eat a balanced meal. This means that the meal should contain *protein, carbohydrates, fats, vitamins, minerals,* and *fiber.*

Advertising also influences our choice of foods. Advertisements on television or in magazines may show new dishes that a food company wants to sell, or established lines which must continue to sell. We are often encouraged by advertisements to try new foods rather than eating those we already know.

Attractively presented food tempts us to try it. This ship's steward looks proud of the appetizing spread he is ready to serve to passengers.

Special occasions

When we want to celebrate, we often have a special meal and share the occasion with other people. On their birthday, many children have a special party to which they invite all their friends. The high point of that party is the meal: sandwiches, ice cream, and a special birthday cake with candles on top. A once-a-year treat.

Enjoying a good meal has always been a way of marking a special day. A festival was originally a day set aside for feasting. How many religious festivals can you think of?

Perhaps the most widely celebrated religious feast is that of Christmas. In most parts of this country, Christmas falls at that time of the year when the weather is cold. So, the traditional Christmas dinner is a hearty meal—hot turkey with stuffing, potatoes and vegetables, followed by fruit cake, and perhaps mince pie with whipped cream. Whenever possible,

Above *These Turkish women have gathered for a special feast to celebrate a wedding.*

all the family—aunts and uncles, grandmothers and grandfathers—gather together, perhaps for the only time in the year, to enjoy this special occasion. Some families may eat this meal in the middle of the day, but others prefer to have Christmas dinner in the evening.

Different people throughout the world celebrate their own special occasions, not always of a religious kind. At the center of nearly all these celebrations is a special meal.

Left *A birthday party in England is an occasion for favorite foods like sausages on sticks, crisps, and cakes.*

Eating out

Most people, at some time or other, eat meals away from their home. This can be for any one of a number of reasons: perhaps the most common reason for eating out is that we are celebrating some special occasion. But people also eat out through necessity—when they are away from home, when they have not had the chance to buy food to cook themselves, or when they would like to eat types of food which they are unable to cook themselves.

There are many reasons for eating out and many different places to eat in. These range from the relatively cheap to the very expensive, and from those serving the simplest to those serving the most exotic types of food. There are snack bars serving sandwiches, cakes, and simple meals for those in a hurry. There are cafes serving fried food, hamburger restaurants, and pizzerias. You can eat a more formal three-course meal, served by waiters or waitresses, in a traditional restaurant. Today there are many restaurants serving foreign food such as Italian, French, and Chinese. How many different types of foreign restaurants do you have in your town?

Enjoying a meal in different surroundings, which someone else has cooked for you, is a pleasant way to spend an evening out.

How food is preserved

Many years ago people could eat food only when it was fresh, because it quickly went bad if it was left too long. Now we have many ways of keeping food for a long time. Keeping food cold is one way of preserving it. A cool refrigerator will keep food for an extra few days, but a freezer can keep it for months. Another method is to dry food; this is how raisins, currants, and prunes are all preserved. Food can also be salted, smoked, or pickled. Think of the many types of pickled vegetables that are sold in the shops.

Perhaps the most important method of keeping food is by putting it in cans. This is a safe way of keeping food edible, often for years.

In the summer there is plenty of fruit and vegetables to eat, and this is the time when people are busy preserving food for the winter when little is growing. The peas that you eat with a meal in winter will have been picked in summer, and frozen, canned, or dried within a day or so. Because of this, you can eat peas six months later, long after the farmers have picked their last crop.

In many poor countries, food is preserved by drying and salting. In southern Africa, strips of meat are preserved by drying. These are called *biltong*. In Asia, people who live by rivers and near the sea eat dried fish. After the fish are caught,

Right *Packing broccoli prior to freezing.*

Left *Drying fish called Bombay Duck in an Indian fishing village.*

they are cleaned, the heads are removed, and they are hung up to dry in the sun.

Before meat is dried, it is often soaked in brine. Brine is water with salt in it. For many centuries, people have known that salt prevents the growth of many of the bacteria that cause food to go bad.

How and where we buy food

When we want to buy food, there are many different types of stores that we can go to. In big cities, there is the small corner shop that sells a variety of goods. It is usually close to home, but it may be expensive. A row of shops close to a local bus stop or train station may also offer a variety of products. There could be a baker selling bread, a butcher selling meat, a grocer selling fruit and vegetables, as well as a vendor selling newspapers and a druggist who makes up prescriptions for medicines. These stores are useful for everyday shopping

Right *This supermarket has its own in-store bakery.*

Left *Stocking up at a small village shop in England.*

but may not be large enough to stock everything that we may want.

The supermarket is where we can buy in large amounts and where we can find all sorts of food under one roof. Even larger are shopping centers, where not only food is on sale but also clothes, toys, kitchen equipment, tools, paint, and many other goods.

Both supermarkets and shopping centers make shopping easier. They usually have large parking lots, so you do not have to carry what you buy very far. You can buy most of your food without trudging from store to store. These stores buy their stocks in such large quantities, that they are able to obtain them at a discount price from the manufacturers. So, the supermarkets can offer their goods to the customers at a lower price than the smaller stores.

Breaking the code

Food does not stay fresh forever and will rot if it is kept too long. So, many food manufacturers (people who make or process food in factories) have for some time marked the labels on their products with a date code. Some of these codes are straightforward dates by which the product must be sold (sell-by dates). But others are secret codes which only the manufacturer and sometimes the storekeeper can understand. These are useful only if a customer makes a complaint to the manufacturer about the quality of a particular item of food. The manufacturer can tell by the code when the food was packaged and on which machine in his factory.

Little by little this secret coding is being replaced by what is called date marking. It is hoped that eventually it will be compulsory for most perishable foods to be marked with the date by which they are best sold or eaten.

Canned and dried food lasts longer than food packed fresh into jars or cartons. Even so, manufacturers press a code into the base of the tin can. Then, if someone returns a can of food which has turned bad, he can trace the batch of food by referring to the code. In such an event, the rest of the batch will be recalled from the stores they have been sold to. This prevents possible illness among other people who have bought cans of the same food, which may also be bad. Some canned foods, too, have begun carrying date markings in recent years.

It is especially important that perishable goods like these are marked with a sell-by date, so the customer can be sure he is buying fresh food.

2 · What people in other countries eat

This map shows you the countries that we are going to look at in this chapter.

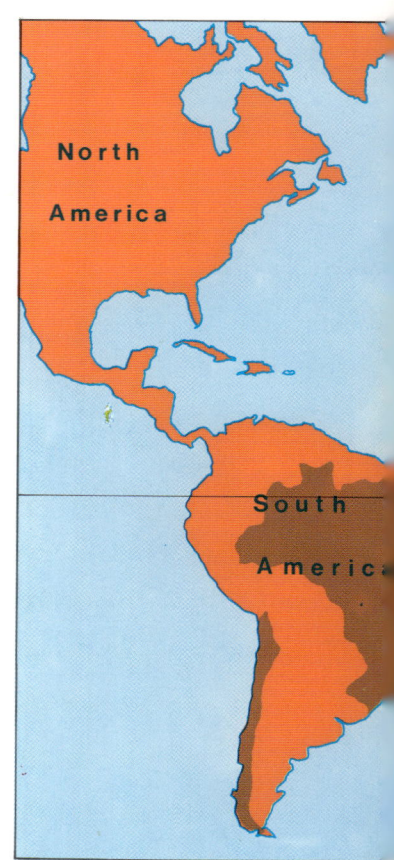

As the sun goes down around the world, people prepare and eat their evening meal. What they will eat and when they will eat depend upon the types of food available and the customs which surround their cooking and eating habits. The climate, geography, and wealth of a country all affect what its people eat.

In many African countries, people will have spent a large part of their day searching for their food. For them, meat is expensive, so their meal will consist mainly of beans or rice. But in the United States, meat is plentiful and relatively cheap. There, people will be sitting down to a juicy steak or a well-garnished hamburger. Some people are further restricted by religious or social taboos. Jews must not eat pork, and, to the native of India, the cow is sacred, so beef must never be eaten.

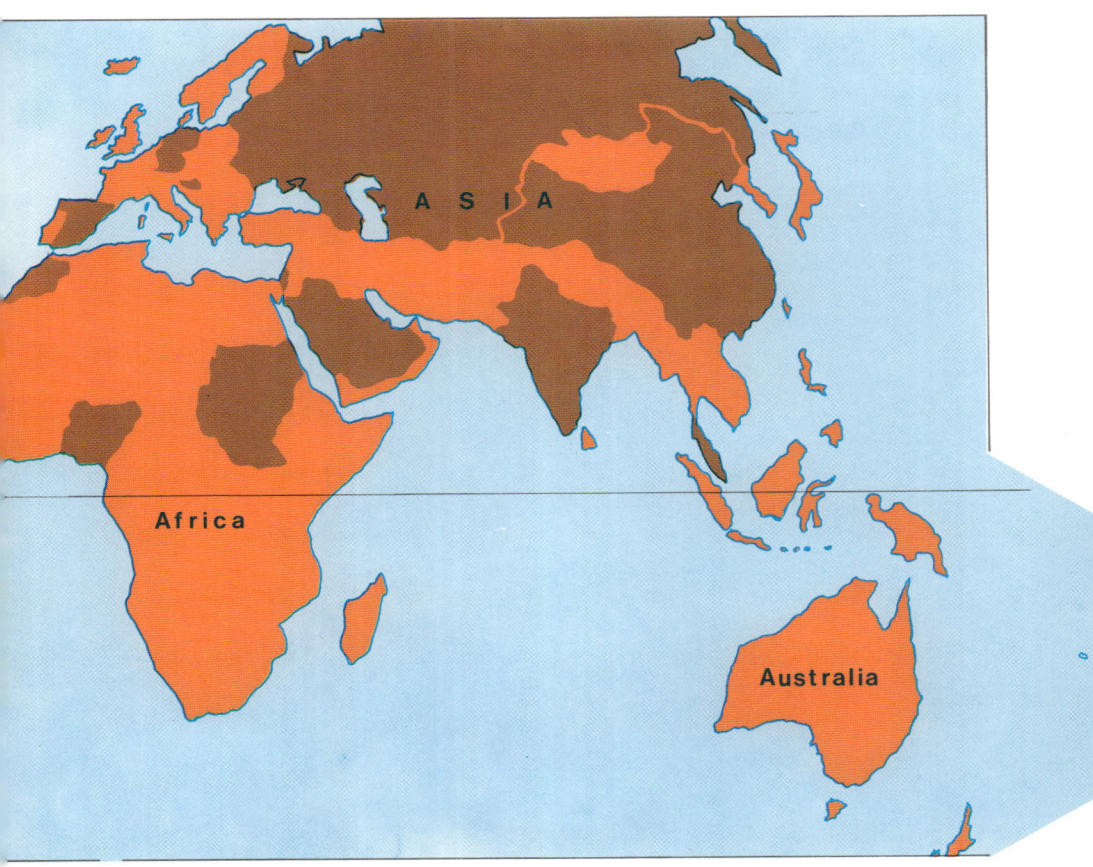

EUROPE
Germany

Germans eat richer, heavier food than do the people in many other Western European countries. Their vegetables are not just boiled and served plain, but are eaten with plenty of butter or a sauce. There are many different types of dumplings, ranging from the delicate little *Spätzle* ('little sparrows') of Swabia to the substantial liver dumplings of Bavaria. These are served with roasts, stews, and soups.

Cooking varies from region to region. In the north, served by the fishermen of Germany's North Sea ports, the people eat much seafood—smoked herring, eels, and mussels. They also enjoy the smoked hams and pork sausages for which they have become famous.

In the south of Germany, pork is cooked in various ways. It is often served with *sauerkraut*—cooked pickled cabbage—and thick sausages, or spit-roasted and served with dumplings.

The people of Berlin have been influenced by Eastern Euro-

Left *A traditional German meal—roast meat, dumplings, sauerkraut, and salad.*

Above *The whole family has gathered for this meal. Father carves the joint of roast meat.*

pean styles of cooking, and are well known for many dishes made from minced meat. They might eat a dinner of poached meatballs in a sauce, or fried meatballs served with grated potato cakes fried in oil, or a hot meat loaf.

Dessert is usually one of the sweet pastries or cakes for which the Germans are famous. If these are a little rich, the family might enjoy some stewed apples instead.

Most German families eat their evening meal quite early. Many fathers start work at 6 A.M. and return home hungry in the late afternoon.

Hungary

The food of Hungary is smooth and warming. Many of the sauces in which Hungarians cook their meat contain cream, and both meat and fish dishes are flavored with sweet pepper, or paprika, as the Hungarians call it. Paprika can be mild, medium, or hot, so the Hungarian cook can select the strength of pepper to suit the dish he or she is flavoring.

Paprika is a vital ingredient in Hungary's national dish, *goulash*. At the end of a cold day, many families sit down to a warming meal of goulash made with either beef or pork with potatoes, onions, paprika, and, perhaps, tomatoes. With the addition of some good stock, the goulash is turned into a hearty soup, often served with bite-sized dumplings.

Hungary produces good wheat, so fresh bread is eaten with most meals. As in most Northern and Eastern European countries, the potato is a common accompaniment to both meat and fish. When potatoes are not served, pasta usually takes their place.

We usually think of pasta and salami as Italian food. Salami is a firm, spiced pork sausage which is sliced and eaten cold. However, outside Italy you will find no finer salami than that made by the Hungarian pork butchers.

Although Hungary has no seacoast and therefore does not have a plentiful supply of fish, the fish from its freshwater rivers and lakes are among the best in Europe.

A tasty goulash *will warm you up on a cold day.*

Spain

Spanish cooking varies from region to region. The peasants living on the arid plains of central Spain had to make the best of whatever food was at hand. Scraps of meat, vegetables, the odd sausage—all found their way into the same pot, to make tasty stews, or *cocidos*, as the Spanish call them. Each region produced its own *cocido*, set apart from any other by the unique combination of local ingredients.

It was in just this way that Spain's national dish, *paella*, which has rice as its main ingredient, came into being. During their 700-year occupation of Spain, the Moors had planted rice fields in the Albufera region of Valencia. They had also brought with them the spices of the East. So the people of Valencia combined the rice and exotic saffron—a spice from the crocus plant—with the abundant seafood of their Mediterranean coastline. Chicken, rabbit, pork, ham, liver, and the spicy Spanish sausage, *chorizo*, may also be added. Paella also contains tomatoes, peas, and beans.

Right *A colorful display of sausages hanging outside a shop in Pamplona.*

Left *Spain's most famous national dish*—paella.

If they are not eating a hearty *cocido* or a *paella* for their evening meal, a Spanish family might start with a soup, continue with a vegetable or meat course, usually containing tomatoes, garlic, and olive oil. The meal is completed with either fresh fruit or a typically Spanish dessert. This would usually be a very sweet concoction, often containing almonds, another legacy from the Moors.

Most families do not eat their evening meal until late, often not before ten o'clock.

Soviet Union

The Soviet Union is made up of many regions. Across its vast expanse, the way of cooking and the types of food eaten change with the changing climate. It is perhaps in the capital city of Moscow that we can find the best examples of typical Soviet cooking.

Life in Russia before the Revolution of 1917 was very hard for all but the rich. Soup was the staple diet of the Russian peasant.

Even today a family in Moscow will start its evening meal with soup—the ever-popular peasant soup of cabbage, *shchi*, or perhaps the deep-red *borscht*, a soup made from beets. The meat course which follows will be served with plenty of vegetables, among them nearly always potatoes. Another way the Moscow housewife might make a little meat go further is to use it in one of the many kinds of meat-filled dumplings that are a popular dish. Bread will always accompany the meal.

If there is no cheese to follow the main course, there could be buckwheat pancakes served with sour cream.

Pancakes are a traditional Russian food. They are served with fish, caviar, butter, sour cream, cream, milk, jam, or honey.

MIDDLE EAST
Israel

Cooking in Israel is as varied as the population itself. Jews have come from all over the world to settle there, and have brought with them the cooking of many lands. You will find the *kebabs* and *baklava* (sweet pastries filled with nuts and honey) of Turkey; the *schnitzel* (thin slices of meat, especially veal) of Germany and Austria. From Eastern Europe there are dumplings, and from America, steaks and hamburgers.

The Jewish religion states that all food must be *kosher*—prepared according to certain rules. Pork, rabbit, and shellfish are forbidden. Meat must not be cooked in milk.

An evening meal in Israel may begin with a sweet fruit soup made with sour cream, a speciality of Russian cooking. This would probably be followed by a chicken or turkey dish, for poultry has become the basis of Israeli meat cooking. A vegetable dish such as eggplant cooked with onions and tomatoes will be served with it.

Special foods are eaten on the Sabbath and at Passover. On the Sabbath there will be a plaited bread topped with poppy seeds called *challah*. For Passover there are special biscuits, honey cake, almond pudding, and unleavened bread to eat.

Above A New Year celebratory meal on a kibbutz.

Left Many varieties of fruit grow in Israel's warm climate. This roadside shop in Jericho sells a good selection.

Saudi Arabia

The evening meal in Saudi Arabia follows the customs of Islam. Before eating, people wash their hands. They then sit cross-legged on cushions on the floor to eat their meal off low, round dining tables. All those at the table must say 'In the name of God,' much as we might say grace. The meal ends with 'To God be thanks.'

Traditionally, Saudis do not eat with knives and forks. Instead, food is picked up by hand, but only the right hand must be used. To be polite, an Arab will eat with only three fingers, licking them when he has finished his meal.

Arab cooking is restricted by the rules of the Islamic religion. Moslems are forbidden to eat meat from the pig, and to drink alcohol. During the month-long religious festival of

Left *Only the right hand is used to eat. The men here are enjoying a meal of lamb and rice.*

Above *Brewing up evening tea over the camp fire.*

Ramadan, Moslems must not eat or drink anything at all during the daytime.

Until recently, lamb and mutton were the only meats available in the *soukhs* (markets) of Saudi Arabia, and these could often be afforded only by the wealthy. The poor made do with beans and lentils. Now the supermarkets of modern Riyadh and Jiddah sell beef and veal—but never pork!

The main course of an evening meal might consist of grilled lamb served with a dish of rice decorated with hard-boiled eggs and fried eggplant. Vegetables are considered to be an important part of the meal, so a main course dish might be eggplant or zucchini squash stuffed with minced lamb, rice, tomato, and parsley. Whatever the dish, it will be eaten with the flat, unleavened bread familiar throughout the Middle East. Dessert will be something sweet, with raisins, honey, and almonds flavoring many of the delicacies, or perhaps fruit.

AFRICA
Sudan

Spiced coffee finishes the meal. It is poured through a straining plug of grass.

Geographically, Sudan is between the Middle East and Africa. Both these countries have affected the everyday life of the Sudanese people. For many years Sudan lived under Anglo-Egyptian rule, and Sudanese cooking reflects the influence of Middle Eastern tastes.

The majority of Sudan's population is Moslem, and its eating habits are governed by the same religious restrictions as those of its neighbor across the Red Sea, Saudi Arabia. All Moslems are taught that travelers are welcome guests at any meal. However, the rules of Islam must be followed: men and women

A crowd of interested spectators gathers around a slaughtered cow.

cannot sit down to eat together.

A typical evening meal will consist of a thick stew made from dried meat, beans, tomatoes, onions, and garlic. This is served on a large tray and is eaten with *kista*, which is flat unleavened bread. Each mouthful of stew is wrapped in bread and then dropped into the mouth.

Dessert might be just a bowl of ground rice served with fruit juice. It will be followed by spiced coffee. To make this, the coffee beans are first roasted over a fire and crushed. Spices and boiling water are then added. Before pouring the coffee, a bundle of grass is pushed into the spout of the pot to act as a strainer. This is served with candies more typical of the Middle East than of Africa.

Nigeria

The evening meal in Nigeria is eaten in the cool of dusk, when the sun has gone down and everyone has finished his or her work for the day. It will be the main meal of the day for most Nigerians. Meat is expensive in Nigeria, so much use is made in cooking of beans, nuts, and fruit. In the villages, meals are cooked over an open fire. Only in the big cities, such as Lagos, are stoves used.

Nigerians like their food hot and spicy. Their slang word for food is *chop*. For their evening meal, they might eat palm oil chop, which is chicken or beef fried in palm oil and served with rice, onions, and other vegetables. Nigeria grows large crops of groundnuts, or peanuts, and sells them all over the world. Nigerians use these to make a hearty dinner of groundnut stew, with either meat or fish and flavored with onions and ginger. Groundnuts may also be made into cakes and fried in palm oil.

Dessert might be fruit in season—mangoes, pineapples, pawpaws, and juicy green-skinned oranges—or it might be a creamy banana and coconut pudding, which can be eaten either hot or cold.

Left *Grilling meat on skewers arranged around a fire.*

Right *Two yam sellers stand proudly, surrounded by a heap of their wares.*

Morocco

The people of Morocco have been Moslems for over a thousand years, so it is not surprising that the food of the Moroccan people is more similar to that of Arabia than of Africa.

For evening meal, there may be a spicy *tagine*, a stew made with cubes of lamb and onions and flavored with saffron, coriander, ginger, and fruit—quinces, dates, raisins, or prunes. *Kebabs*, which are made by pushing cubes of meat such as mutton, liver, kidney, or beef sausage onto a skewer, are popular. When cooked, the meat is taken off the skewer and put into a *kesrah*—a flat, round bread roll which has been cut open. A sauce is then poured over it. On a special occasion there may be *bstilla*, a crisp pie made up of layers of fine semolina pastry alternating with pigeon meat, spices, and sugar, which is fried instead of baked.

Desserts often contain honey and almonds, perhaps in a pancake, or served with semolina. Refreshing mint tea finishes the meal.

Left *Corn drying on village roofs high in the Atlas Mountains.*

Right *A man climbs a date palm to pick some fruit. Dates are used in both sweet and savory dishes.*

ASIA
India

There are several different styles of cooking in India, which come from the traditional cookery of the top caste in that particular area. There are also influences of other peoples who have invaded India in the past. But what each family eats may vary enormously, depending on religion, caste, and how wealthy it is.

In the north of the country, meat is a common sight at the evening meal. Usually mutton or chicken, it can be roasted in a clay oven, a *tandoor*, minced and served as spicy meatballs, grilled in the form of kebabs, or braised in a yogurt sauce. Dishes in this part of the country are generally drier than those served in the south. The staple diet of the north is wheat, but in the south more rice is served with meals, and this absorbs the wetter curry sauces that give flavor and variety to mainly vegetarian dishes.

Above *Shopping for the herbs and spices that are an important part of Indian cooking.*

There are no separate courses. All the dishes that make up the evening meal will be placed in little bowls around the *chapatties*—unleavened bread—or rice. There may be two or three vegetable dishes, one of which will be a *dhal*, a pulse (seed) such as lentil, a meat or fish dish, and a selection of pickles and chutneys (relishes). The family eat with their fingers from the bowls.

Whether meat or vegetarian, Indian cookery is rich in spices. These not only add flavor and variety to dishes, but also serve to preserve the food in India's hot climate.

Of course, many millions of Indians are too poor to eat such a large meal. They may only be able to afford a thin soup, or a piece of sugarcane to chew.

Left *Cooking a curry for the family's evening meal.*

Malaysia

Less than half the population of Malaysia are of the Malayan race. By far the largest racial group are the Chinese, but there are also many people who have crossed the sea from India to live there. So, the eating habits of the Malaysians reflect the cooking of both China and India as well as that of the Malays, whose cooking is found in a purer form in Indonesia.

The Malaysian family sits down in the cool of evening to eat the main meal of the day. Many of the dishes will be hot and spicy, like those found in both India and Indonesia, and will be served with either rice or noodles. The main dish might be pancakes stuffed with meat, vegetables, or fish, for the coastlines of Malaysia are extensive and rich in fish and seafood. Fish curry and shrimp paste salad are popular dishes. There might also be a salad of cooked and raw vegetables served in a peanut sauce.

If the savory dishes have been spicy, dessert might be a soothing chilled custard made with dried coconut.

Right *Many Chinese people live in Malaya. This stall is selling special food during the Chinese New Year festival.*

Left *A man cooks a tasty meal for his family.*

China

No cooking is more inventive than that of China. The Chinese cook has one aim: to please the senses of those who eat his or her food. Chinese families usually eat an early evening meal—between 5:30 and 7:30. The meal is made up of many dishes, which are carefully chosen to provide a range of different flavors, textures, and colors. Some may be sweet—like sweet and sour pork, and some may be salty—like fried rice. Other well-known Chinese dishes which you may have tried: *chow mein*, pancake rolls (*dim sums*), and *chop suey*. Meat, vegetables, and fish are cut into small pieces and

Above A Western guest proposes a toast to his Chinese friends during the meal.

quick-fried, steamed, or casseroled.

Chopsticks—thin pieces of polished wood or plastic—are used to eat with. Each person dips his chopsticks into the various dishes. Every mouthful is followed by some rice from each person's individual bowl. Soup is not eaten at the beginning of the meal, but during it, to refresh the taste buds! There is tea to drink with the meal, and instead of bread there are steamed or baked pancakes. Most people do not eat a dessert, but if they do, it may be fruit such as lychees.

Left A Chinese meal combines a great variety of dishes.

SOUTH AMERICA
Chile

Chileans eat their evening meal very late, at about ten o'clock. It may not be the main meal of the day, for many people eat a large lunch before they take their afternoon siesta. The evening meal is often a social affair, with friends gathering together to share their news.

Meat is barbecued or cooked in stews, or in *cazuela*, the popular soup of meat, vegetables, rice, and corn. Seafood is popular everywhere. The country's coastline is some 4,000 km (2,600 miles) long and the average width of the land is only 177 km (110 miles). Favorite seafood dishes which might be cooked for the evening meal include giant sea urchins, either served raw or as a filling in pancakes, and *paila*, a seafood stew. There are over fifty varieties of shellfish for the cook to choose from.

After the main course, most people eat a simple dessert of fresh fruit. This might include the custard apple, which grows in the north of the country and is often pulped, sweetened, mixed with water, and served as a cool refreshing drink.

Right *A little girl dives into* cazuela, *a soup of meat, corn, rice, and vegetables.*

Left *A Santiago grocery shop. Fresh fruit is a popular dessert.*

Brazil

The population of Brazil is made up of many different races, so there are many different styles of cooking. Portuguese food and Italian dishes such as pizza and spaghetti are popular, but you may also find African and American Indian dishes.

Black beans and rice are the main ingredients in most Brazilian dishes, and can be found in the country's national dish, *fejoada completa*. Every housewife has her own recipe for this dish and spends hours combining the many ingredients that give it its special flavor. Most recipes include black beans, rice, dried beef, smoked tongue, bacon, sausage, and the ears, feet, and tail of a pig. This is served on special occasions.

A boy finishes his meal with a mango.

A fisherman roasts his catch in a flooded forest by the Amazon River.

Many main course dishes are made from a mixture of beans, rice, and meat. Those may be served with *farofa* (cassava flour mixed with bacon, eggs, and olives) and a salad. In the south of the country, meat barbecued on skewers is popular.

A large variety of fruit is grown in Brazil and many of these—bananas, oranges, pineapples, passionfruit, mangoes, guavas, melons, custard apples, and apricots—are made into ice cream. Either fresh fruit or ice cream provides a refreshing dessert to end a rich meal. And after the meal, as throughout the day, cups of strong, black, sweet coffee are served. Brazil grows a large amount of coffee, which is exported all over the world.

Recipes

FRIED RICE
from China

Ingredients:
300g (10oz) boiled rice
2 onions
2 eggs
100g (4oz) chopped pork
1 tablespoon chopped parsley
2 tablespoons soy sauce
oil for frying
pinch of salt and pepper

Equipment:
chopping board
knife
whisk
bowl
saucepan
spoon

1. Chop onions and beat eggs in a small bowl.
2. Heat oil in pan and fry the rice.
3. Add onions, pork, salt, and pepper.
4. When mixed, make a hole in the center and put in the eggs. When eggs are almost cooked, stir in the rice from sides of the pan.
5. Add parsley and soy sauce.

ALMOND PUDDING
from Israel

Ingredients:
100g (4oz) ground almonds
75g (3oz) castor sugar
4 eggs

Equipment:
2 large bowls
whisk
wooden spoon
baking tray

1. Separate the yolks and the whites of the eggs.
2. Whisk whites to a stiff froth.
3. Beat yolks and sugar together till light and frothy.
4. Add ground almonds and beaten egg white. Beat for another five minutes.
5. Turn into greased baking tray. Bake at 325°F/160°C for fifty minutes.
6. Serve cold, sprinkled with castor sugar.

TOMATE TOREADOR
from Spain

Ingredients:
4 hard boiled eggs
2 teaspoons chopped
  chives, 1 of chopped
  parsley, 1 of chopped
  onion
2 tablespoons bread crumbs
1 clove garlic
50g (2oz) butter
12 tomatoes
oil for frying

Equipment:
chopping board
knife
fork
bowl
small pan
wire basket
frying pan

1. Mash eggs with a fork and put into a bowl.
2. Add chives, parsley, onions, and bread crumbs.
3. Crush the garlic and add to bread crumb mixture.
4. Melt butter in a pan and add to eggs and bread crumb mixture. Mix thoroughly.
5. Cut tomatoes in half and take out the pulp and seeds.
6. Fill tomato shells with egg and bread crumb mixture.
7. Put in wire basket and fry quickly in hot oil.

RICE BISCUITS
from India

Ingredients:
225g (8oz) ground rice
112g (4oz) butter
150ml (¼ pint) milk
225g (8oz) sugar
1 teaspoon nutmeg
salt to taste

Equipment:
mixing bowl
knife
rolling pin
biscuit cutter
baking tray

1. Mix butter and ground rice; add the sugar, salt dissolved in a little water, nutmeg powder, and milk.
2. Knead to a stiff dough.
3. Roll out dough to biscuit thickness.
4. Cut to required size with biscuit cutter.
5. Place the biscuits on a buttered tray and bake at 190°C/375°F until golden brown.

3 · Food for life: hygiene

To make sure that the food we eat is safe and free from germs, everything in the kitchen must be kept clean. This is called hygiene. First we must keep ourselves clean when we cook. Our hands must be washed, nails cleaned, and bandages or tape put on any cuts we may have. In this way, we can stop dirt and germs getting into our food from our hands.

Next we must be sure that the kitchen and the equipment we shall be using are quite clean. All work surfaces should be carefully wiped, the floor swept, any spilled food cleaned up. Cloths which we are going to use to dry utensils should also be clean. There is little point in cleaning a plate and then making it dirty by drying it with a soiled cloth.

Lastly, we should make sure that our food is safe to eat. If we are using fresh food, we must check that no parts of it have gone bad, that the meat is not dark and moldy and that fruit and vegetables are not rotten. It is dangerous to cook food that is no longer fresh. Canned and packaged food should be kept in a clean cupboard and well sealed so that flies and other insects cannot contaminate the contents of the packages.

If we do not follow these rules, we could make ourselves or someone else who eats our food very ill with food poisoning.

It is important to keep ourselves and our cooking utensils clean when preparing food.

Feast and famine

About two thirds of the world's population live in 'the developing countries,' often called the Third World. These are poor countries where most people do not have enough to eat. Most of Africa, Asia, and South America have food problems. But some countries have more than enough for their people to eat—most of Europe, Canada, the United States, Australia, and New Zealand. Some countries produce such a large amount of certain foods that there is plenty for their own people and enough left over to sell to other countries. The U.S.A., Canada, and Australia sell wheat; New Zealand and Australia export lamb and beef. In Europe, many of the Mediterranean countries sell fruit and vegetables.

In Asia and Africa, some countries always have to buy food to stop people from starving, but they have very little to sell in return. Frequently there are natural disasters such as droughts, when there is no rain at all. Then the crops die and

The horrific results of starvation.

Cambodian children queue for rice at a refugee camp.

there is a famine. Many people die from starvation. Today the world has a population of about 4.5 billion people. The United Nations says that 1.3 billion people do not have enough to eat—and 500 million of these people are suffering from starvation.

As the world's population continues to grow, the problem of providing enough food for everyone gets worse. We have to investigate methods of increasing food production and sharing food fairly among everybody.

The results of eating

There are many people whose work it is to provide us with food. There are farmers and farmworkers who grow the food; factory workers who make cakes, biscuits, and bread; butchers and grocers who sell us meat and vegetables; and chefs, waiters, and waitresses who prepare and serve our food. But what happens to the waste once we have eaten our food and it has passed through our digestive system?

Once we flush our toilets, the waste passes down a drain and is carried underground. The drains from all the toilets on your street or area join into one very large drain. This system is called the sewage system, and most people who live in towns and cities use it. The waste from the toilets of people who live in the country goes into a septic tank—a large underground tank, usually in the yard. A special tank truck is used to empty the septic tank. The waste from both the sewage system and these special tankers is taken to sewage disposal plants.

At the sewage plant, the liquids and solids are separated in

Left Litter — containers once used for food become a problem when empty.

Right These 'bacteria beds' are a simple filtration system at the sewage works.

large tanks. The solids fall to the bottom so that the liquid can run into overflow pipes. Once they have been separated, the solids are dried and can be used in fertilizers to enrich the soil. The liquid goes through many cleaning cycles. It does not become pure water, but many of its impurities are removed. When the liquid has been treated, it is disposed of in streams and rivers.

Glossary

BALANCED DIET   To eat different foods which will provide the body with all the nutriments necessary for good health.

BARBECUE   A meal cooked out of doors on an open fire.

BRINE   Salt and water mixed together. It is used to preserve food.

BSTILLA   Pigeon pie made in Morocco.

CARBOHYDRATES   Potatoes, bread, cake, and cookies are all in this group of food. Carbohydrates give us energy and keep us warm.

CASTE   The Hindu class system.

CHOP   Nigerian word for food.

CHOPSTICKS   A pair of thin sticks held together in one hand to pick up food, especially in Japan, Taiwan, and China.

CRUMPETS   A light soft yeast cake full of small holes on the top side, eaten toasted and buttered.

DIGESTIVE SYSTEM   This is the name given to the different parts of our bodies which change food into a form that can be used by the body.

FEJOADA   Brazilian meat dish.

FIBER   Foods containing fiber help to keep your digestive system working properly. Most fruit and vegetables are in this group, as well as whole meal bread.

GOULASH   Hungarian meat dish flavored with sweet pepper.

KEBABS   Meat and vegetables placed on a skewer and grilled.

KISTA   Thin pancake bread made in Sudan.

KOSHER   A special way of preparing and cooking food found in Israel and among Jewish people throughout the world.

PAELLA   A Spanish dish made of rice, meat, and seafood.

PASSOVER   An eight-day Jewish festival which commemorates the sparing of the Israelites in Egypt.

PIZZERIA   A restaurant serving pizzas.

PRESERVING   This stops meat and vegetables from going bad quickly.

PROTEIN   Meat, fish, eggs, cheese, and nuts are all part of the protein group of foods. These are essential body-building foods.

SAUERKRAUT   Pickled cabbage eaten in Germany and Eastern Europe.

STAPLE DIET   The main food of a country's people. If it lacks essential protein, vitamins, and minerals, it will cause the people who rely on it to become malnourished.

UNLEAVENED BREAD   Bread that is made without yeast and so does not rise and become light and springy. It stays flat like a pancake.

VITAMINS AND MINERALS   Substances found in certain foods, which are essential to good health. We only need a small amount of them every day.

Finding out more

The following organizations may be able to help with information on various foods, aspects of diet, or meals around the world.

American Institute of Nutrition, 9650 Rockville Pike, Bethesda, MD 20814
4-H Clubs Extension Service, U.S. Department of Agriculture, Washington D.C. 20250
Future Farmers of America, Box 15160, Alexandria, VA 22309
Future Homemakers of America, 2010 Massachusetts Ave. NW, Washington D.C. 20036
National Association of Food Processors, 1133 20th Street NW, Washington D.C. 20036
National Dairy Council, 6300 North River Road, Rosemont, IL 60013
National Health Council, 70 W. 40th St., New York, New York
Public Health Association of America, 1015 15th Street NW, Washington D.C.
U.S. Committee for World Health, 777 United Nations Plaza, New York, NY 10017
World Health Organization, Avenue Appia 1211, Geneva 27, Switzerland

Index

Advertising 11
Africa 16, 23, 36, 37, 38, 39, 40, 41, 50, 56
Almond pudding recipe 52
Almonds 29, 32, 35, 40

Baked beans 6
Baklava 32
Balanced meal 11
Barbecue 4, 5, 51
Beans 9, 23, 29, 35, 37, 38, 50
Beef 23, 26, 35, 38, 40, 50, 56
Biltong 16
Borscht 31
Brazil 50, 51
Bread 6, 18, 26, 31, 32, 35, 37, 40, 43, 47, 58
Bstilla 40

Cakes 6, 7, 12, 14, 25, 32, 58
Canned food 16, 20
Carbohydrates 11
Caste 42
Cazuela 49
Challah 32
Chapatties 43
Cheese 9, 31
Chile 48, 49
China 14, 45, 46, 47
Chopsticks 47
Chop suey 46
Chorizo 29
Chow mein 46
Christmas 12, 13
Cocidos 28, 29
Coconut 38, 45
Coffee 36, 37, 51
Cream 26, 30, 31, 32
Curry 9, 42, 45

Date coding 20, 21
Dessert 6, 9, 25, 29, 32, 35, 37, 38, 40, 45, 47, 49, 51
Dinner 8, 9
Dried food 16, 17, 20, 37

Dumplings 24, 26, 31, 32

Eggs 6, 35, 51

Farofa 51
Fats 11
Fejoada completa 50
Festivals 12, 13, 32, 33, 34, 45
Fiber 11
Fish 6, 11, 17, 24, 26, 28, 30, 38, 43, 45, 46, 49, 51
Freezing food 16, 17
Fried rice recipe 52
Fruit 9, 16, 18, 25, 29, 32, 35, 38, 40, 41, 47, 48, 49, 56

Germany 24, 25, 32
Goulash 9, 26, 27
Groundnuts 38

Hamburgers 5, 6, 14, 23, 32
High tea 4, 6, 7
Honey 30, 32, 35, 40
Hungary 9, 26, 27
Hygiene 54, 55

Ice cream 6, 12, 51
India 9, 16, 23, 42, 43, 45
Islam 34, 36
Israel 32
Italy 9, 14, 26, 50

Jam 6, 30
Jelly 6, 12
Jews 23, 32

Kebabs 32, 40, 42
Kesrah 40
Kista 37
Kosher food 32

Lamb 34, 35, 40, 56
Lasagna 9

Malaysia 44, 45

63

Meat 4, 8, 11, 12, 17, 18, 23, 24, 26, 28, 29, 31, 32, 34, 35, 37, 38, 40, 42, 43, 45, 46, 49, 50, 54, 58
Milk 6, 30, 32
Minerals 11
Moslems 34, 36, 40
Mutton 35, 40, 42

Nigeria 38, 39
Nuts 29, 32, 38

Paella 28, 29
Paila 49
Pancakes 30, 31, 40, 45, 46, 47, 49
Pasta 9, 26
Pork 23, 24, 26, 28, 32, 34, 35, 46, 50
Potatoes 6, 9, 11, 12, 25, 26, 31
Poultry 12, 28, 32, 38, 42
Preserving food 16, 17, 43
Pudding 6, 9, 25, 29, 32, 35, 37, 38, 40, 47, 49, 51

Restaurants 4, 14, 15
Rice 9, 23, 28, 34, 35, 37, 38, 42, 43, 45, 46, 47, 49, 50, 51
Rice biscuits recipe 53

Salad 6, 24, 45, 51
Salami 26
Sandwiches 6, 12, 14
Saudi Arabia 34, 35, 36
Sauerkraut 24

Sausages 5, 6, 12, 24, 26, 28, 29, 40, 50
Schnitzel 32
Sell-by dates 20, 21
Sewage disposal 58, 59
Shchi 31
Shellfish 24, 28, 32, 45, 49
Shops 18, 19, 20, 35
Soup 24, 26, 29, 31, 32, 43, 47, 49
Soviet Union 30, 31, 32
Spaghetti 6, 50
Spain 28, 29
Special occasions 12, 13, 14, 33
Staple diet 42
Starvation 56, 57
Stews 11, 24, 28, 37, 38, 40, 49
Sudan 36, 37

Tagine 40
Tea 6, 35, 40, 47
Third World 56, 57
Tomate Toreador recipe 53

Unleavened bread 32, 35, 37, 43
U.S.A. 4, 5, 23, 32, 56

Vegetables 8, 11, 12, 16, 17, 18, 24, 26, 28, 29, 31, 32, 35, 38, 39, 43, 45, 46, 49, 54, 56, 58
Vitamins 8, 9, 11

Yogurt 9, 42

Picture acknowledgments

British Egg Information Service 55; J. Allan Cash 10, 18, 21, 29, 32, 38, 39, 40, 41; Rennie Ellis front cover; Elisabeth Photo Library 7, 46; Alan Hutchison Library 16, 35, 42, 43, 44, 47, 48, 49, 50, 51; Malaysian Tourist Corporation 45; MEPHA 13, 34, 36, 37; John Mitchell 22-23; Novosti Press Agency 30; Oxfam 56, 57; Picturepoint 5 (below), 6, 8, 12, 15, 17, 19, 24, 28, 33, 59; John Topham Picture Library 5 (above), 58.

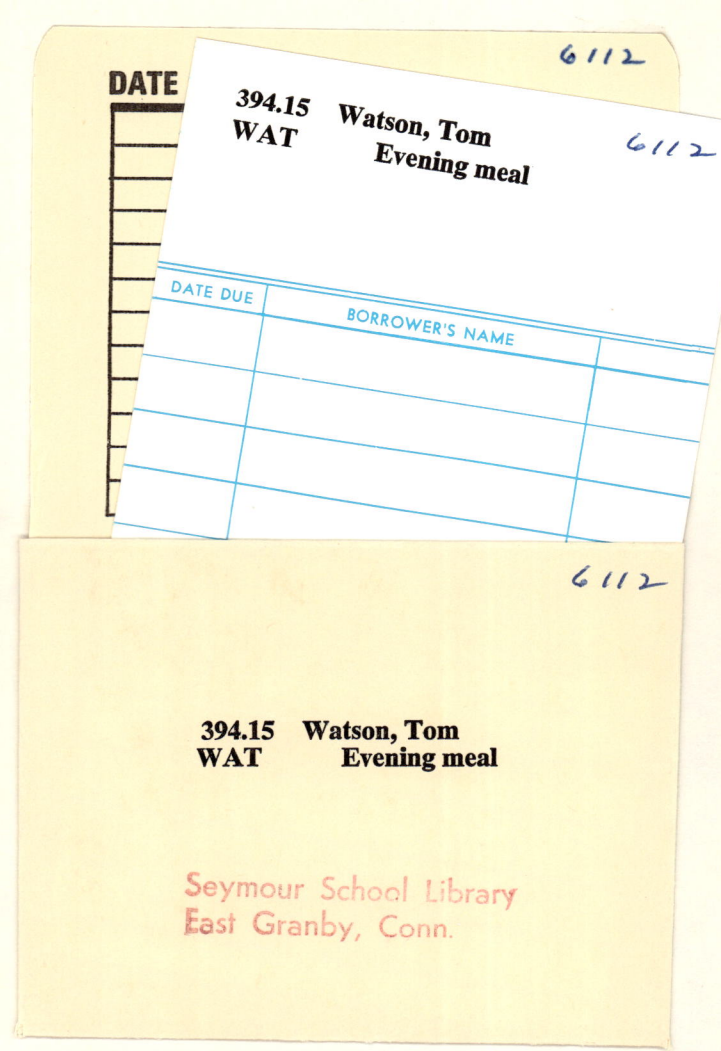